INSIDE OUT

DIONNA OPHELIA

authorHOUSE®

AuthorHouse™
1663 Liberty Drive
Bloomington, IN 47403
www.authorhouse.com
Phone: 1-800-839-8640

Published by AuthorHouse 2/12/2013

ISBN: 978-1-4567-6299-5 (sc)
ISBN: 978-1-4685-6576-8 (e)

Table of Contents

Preface

Not ashamed of the story my life brings

Sharing this with you because I learned some things.

Not glorifying the fruit of sin revealed

Just exposing the truth of things that's real.

This long awaited craft many has been seeking

Has finally been unleashed...Poetically Speaking!

Acknowledgements

VA- NAACP/ James River Journal: Like a bridge over troubled waters. Thank you for support.

CRG: (music man) Talent and brains...un-new to the game... Witness to your tracks being off the chain...Told me to throw it back put a face to the name...Knowing really it's not about the fame...Stand up, Encore..."Inside Out" boomeranged! Thanks for all your inspiration, advise and even telling-it-like-it is when needed.

The Alchemist (Paulo Coelho): This helped to awaken me and shed light in dark areas of my life. Like Santiago, I too shall see my pyramids and behold awaiting treasures........Maktub!!!

Dedications

Thank you Heavenly Father unto this day I pray, you placed the words in my mind and heart to write the things I say. Inspirations and experiences written to help see me through, are God given talents received that I give back to you.

Taeonna (daughter): The Sunshine of my life. Many of days you were all I had. Shine on!

Taylin (son): A glance in your eyes refuels my fire bringing me closer to my purpose. My littleKing!

Elantra (God-daughter): There's truly life within you; Love your energy and strength.....never settle!

Valerie (mom): Thank you for watering your seed even when the sun didn't shine and for those periodic reminders to share this gift with the world.

Marcia (Big Sister): You can't imagine how much admiration I have for you; you've taught me a lot.

Ernest, Darius, Angel, Zahra...I truly love you all...Thanks to family and all those who have inspired and supported my dream. Love, Peace and mayall hatred cease!

Dionna Ophelia (2001, 2006, 2011, 2013)

GENERAL

The Picture I Paint

To: Taeonna

The picture I paint will be pure and clear

The best of hand strokes with no smears.

Some personality here, a touch of class there

Sure to paint love on it everywhere.

So original and flawless I've seen thus far

In the category of an Angel; a shining Star.

The value of this painting could never be priced

It's more precious than gold and sweeter than spice.

This treasured art represents all aspects of truth

You should know by now the picture I painted was you.

<u>To Get Away</u>

Have you ever wanted to get away, far beyond that you know?

With distance being no factor, you definitely would go.

Imagine the title lifted from over your head

Breathing air of the unfamiliar instead.

You awake from a dream to still think you're sleep

Not one meeting or appointment to keep.

No schedule in sight...your time is yours

No cooking, no cleaning or signs of chores.

In a state of mind mentally free

Can't wait to Get Away and just let things be!

Thoughts...Mentally Speaking

I heard a voice breaking through silence, oh who could this be?

Alone, yet the voice is familiar to me.

Thoughts of events today that took place

Thinking of tomorrow as yesterday leaves a trace.

The voice of reason lets the conscience kick in

Correcting the wrongs, struggling to win.

Flashes of those I'm in and out of contact with

Resting, but in my dreams my mind still drifts.

This prevalent voice of mine was inadvertently seeking

Some moments of candid silence to be heard mentally speaking.

Homeless Heart

Here beats a heart with a rhythm unknown

Lost on a path in search of a home

Passing up shelters due to instability

Untouchable heart if you're not feeling me.

Contenders come around I see through them like glass

Unwise words uttered, out of my class.

Watching couples sometimes encourage my desire

Several prospects but their fuel dissipates my fire.

So I continue the journey pacing to each beat

Listening for that kindred rhythm as love takes a seat.

Aware of imitators my heart's at risk

Seldom questioning if this home exists?

Love and time at war as I'm slowly picked apart

Only that destined rhythm can house this Homeless Heart.

<u>One Day</u>

I don't know where I don't know who

I just know now I live without you.

A yearning heart with questions inside

For the flourishing of love, how long will you hide?

Have I seen your face or even come close

My appetite's growing, I long for your dose.

Patience running thin as time continues to pass

For the love my heart desires…One Day…at last!

<u>A Girl Like Me</u>

I don't know where to start so much to say, there aren't enough hours in a day. See a girl like me can't stand being stressed, someone always want a favor, what now let me rest......and don't get a little loot cause they'll come from all around.....that's until my chips are falling down. But a girl like me isn't having that I've learned the hard way so get off my back. What? ...I'm not mad or trying to be rude; just keeping-it-real.....best technique used. See if you're down for me then swing my way.....we can kick it all night and the next day. A girl like me don't come a dime a dozen, so smooth and cool, down with you and your cousin.....got love for all shades cause that what God made and it's all good from the country to the hood. No hating in my playing, man you hear what I'm saying? One love, spread peace, and strive to be free....but don't forget to keep-it-real from a girl like me!

<u>One On One With Cupid</u>

When I sat down to talk with Cupid I saw weary in his eyes as well

He spoke of his perfect aim to the heart but takes the heat when love fails.

It's frustrating dislodging arrows of love and it returns broken in your face

With low spirits he whispered, "It's not me that causes love to be displaced."

For a moment silence emerged seems that Cupid was lost in deep thoughts

Reminiscing on how I've love and lost knowing it wasn't Cupid's fault.

Holding his hand to reassure that his work wasn't in vain

I explained how we'd have unwanted experiences and sometimes severe pain.

The love arrows came from Cupid for lives to be touched

But somehow it got twisted and from hurt didn't mean as much.

<u>Empty Heart</u>

In my bed a body there lies

Meeting physical needs as my soul still cries.

Empty and void a heart one can't claim

All the while loneliness was winning the game.

Hungry for love thirsty for this man

Beyond fantasies for him to take my hand.

Impatience within I can no longer bare

As I seek love from who knows where.

What I'm Made Of

To: Marcia

A mother before giving birth…Weary of evil on this earth

Angers stirs when justice fails…Triggering one to want to raise hell.

Neutral in the midst of the storm…Trying to stay focus, got to move on.

Somewhat down when a loved one is lost…Another tab for the heart's cost.

Glamorous when it's time to chill…Always soul searching that's for real.

I'll fix a hot plate and entertain guest…Always thankful, Lord knows I'm blessed.

Humor helps to keep me alive…Especially when it feels I'm dying inside.

Desiring happiness for all to gain…Aware that the remedy isn't wealth nor fame.

To sum it all up I've got nothing but love…And that's exactly
What I'm Made Of.

My Sorrow, My Pain

At times my laughs are drowned by tears

As I struggle with the fact that you're not here.

And I know in a better place you now rest

Though it's hard depleting this pain in my chest.

Life's walk without you won't be quite the same

As time unfolds I'll get through my Sorrow and Pain.

Negro Tendacies

Negro tendencies culturally embedded in the soul

As a youth its image will start to unfold.

Ever caught the rhythm to a song that you never heard

Or said "yes" in response but didn't hear a word?

You ever used a toothbrush to clean your shoes

Or returned an item after it was used?

Ever made a meal out of hot dogs you know who you are

Or scrambled for loose change to put gas in the car?

How about giving out the wrong number and name

Then comment on how people play games?

You ever tried to get rid of someone by saying you needed space

Or asked for money when you had a stashing place?

Ever spoke to a bill collector and said you weren't home

Or paid enough on a cut-off to keep service on?

If you can say yes in relation to any one of these

Then you've embraced the culture of Negro Tendencies.

With Time

I have been looking for you

Were you trying to find me too?

I've tried to be patient tossing and turning at night

Thought I found love but knew things weren't right.

I pray the warmth in your heart returns on mine

And what we share will blossom and grow forever with time.

<u>If It Wasn't For Poetry</u>

If it weren't for poetry lost energy would flow in my veins

Without a prime outlet to assert my joys and pains.

I'd be somewhat crude like a mouth with no tongue

As if death was at birth before life begun.

My mind.....a weapon and poetry the ammunition

Free diverse expressions, no room for permission.

Creative thoughts of art with a touch of reality

Therapeutic and entertaining with a sense of formality.

So if it weren't for poetry a part of me would be dead

Written emotions enhance life especially when circulated and read.

<u>Who Am I?</u>

I'm known to be pushed away and bluntly neglected

Boldly unwelcome and hard-core rejected.

My sting can be cold leaving one numb

Enhancing grief beyond what the mind succumbs.

My tactics are physical and emotionally felt

I wait to attack when the wrong cards are dealt.

No faith, race or gender can keep me obsolete

As sure as life is given we are sure to meet.

I come with no conscience and put ones through a test

The reminisceof my art leaves many in a mess.

Yes, I am alive and in the evil world I reign

Who am I you may wonder? I'm precisely known as pain.

<u>Don't Let Another Day Go By</u>

Don't let another day go by and we haven't spoken

It may not be visible but my heart is broken.

The silent, distant behaviors are wearing on me

Our relationship is much stronger than this catastrophe.

So I'll put aside me to accept us with open arms

I'm sorry we even went through this....I really meant no harm.

<u>How</u>

How do you go on when answers don't come

And how can I define myself with the partial parent of one?

How can such pain turn to great strength

When the depths of my struggles exceeds its length?

Only in God's name can things get better

I sure hope some answers will come out of this letter.

How can you keep dark thoughts far away

When echoes of memories seem louder some days?

With no direction, how do you know where to turn

Struggling with the remnants of pain's burn?

Though so much anguish I still manage to smile

Signs from above, only Heaven knows How.

<u>Something To Say</u>

This may reach many but most likely not all, aware some won't be resurrected when the trumpet calls. I'll still show concern as my days proceed, giving when I can to those in need. Spreading positive energy and saving some for self, if I let this world drain me there would be no joy in me left. I'll watch the good out one eye and the evil out the other, avoiding hell's chaos so my spirit won't be smothered. Aware of my flaws I try daily to correct, to deny your flaws can diminish your intellect. So many things in life I will never understand like if it's already written than what choice do I have in the plan? That's not a test of my faith for in God I do believe, but some things can change because I used to never wear weave. You probably think I'm tripping and it's been a long day, so I'll count my blessings and get back to you when there's something else to say.

THE UNKNOWN

Peculiar Spirits

An unknown breeze in the still of the wind

A brief moment of chills covers the skin.

Is this breeze refreshing or should I take flight?

As peculiar spirits drift along through the night.

Eternity

As the wind blows and the grass bend

Does our final destination ever end?

Flocked with flames or flying high

Where does life go when the body dies?

Does the light in the tunnel seem to get bright?

Or is it followed by horrible screams of the night?

Where one life leads to the next we'll see

As long as peace follows in Eternity!

Something in the Air

I believe there's something strange in the air…..People blatantly walk by and not speak but stare.

When it comes to driving have people lost their minds…..Careless behind the wheel, in a race against time.

Our children turn to TV for a sense of direction…..This false sense of reality in exchange for rejection.

There's something strange brewing in the air…..It's hovering the skies right here and over there.

Lust is overpowering Love, no commitment in sight…..What we know to be wrong is embraced in the light.

You can't decipher the child from the parents anymore…..No healthy discipline, destruction's in store.

Society's rampage for money and power…..Disrespectful to nature, sinful devours.

Deceitful crimes do anyone care…..A plaque is spreading…. Something's in the Air.

<u>Life of Death</u>

Death isn't evil or something to fear

With each passing day it draws near.

Sometimes it's swift other times slow

The older you get the more it grows.

For certain the living shall meet death

Loss of the physical is life to memories left.

The breath of life can easily be taken

This irreversible transition leaves us shaken.

Do not let death take the joys out of life

Nor take life for granted it may expire in the night.

<u>Friendly Enemies</u>

From my peripheral I see individuals with a knife aimed at my back

Aware of poisons as I avoid being prey to your trap.

Be cautious of the power dwelling within

The knife meant for me may de-flesh your very skin.

For those with good intentions and stood with me thus far

This isn't for you but the two-headed Judas......you know who you are.

<u>Drifting on Troubled Waters</u>

We're living in times when technology is well advanced

But simple doses of high morals we seem not to enhance.

The structure of life and nature is more unbalanced

And the result of most disputes is unfortunate violence.

Mass destruction, bomb threats and even talks of war

Blood is shed daily at home we can't afford more.

Grief and stress taunts our love ones with drugs

Alcohol takes a life as the family pulls the plug.

News warnings, terror alerts and immunizations on the rise

The world different but the same, exploring through uncertain eyes.

Let's not be senseless sons and daughters

Cherish the now as we Drift on Troubled Waters.

Finally Home

Our time together is only borrowed

Cherish memories let there be no sorrow.

My presence I know you'll truly miss

But family and love ones remember this.....

All pain and worries are now far gone

I'm at peace on high, I'm finally home.

LIFE LESSON

Love and Lust

About Life

Forgiveness

Stones

Selfish Love

How Do You Say You're Sorry

Passing Through

Why I Walk Alone

Love Debts

You're Gonna Wish

Silly Me

Familiar Stranger

In My Shoes

I Question Myself

Dear Karma

Karma's Come-Back

Runaway Heart

Love and Lust

Love, absorbed in the body its integrity remains the same

An act or a feeling, a familiar faceless name.

Lust, a false reality of love unknown

A glutton for flesh that vision has shown.

Love embraces passion and the heart is pleased

While lust only meets unemotional needs.

Love and lust, both urges are strong

Lust eventually dies while love last long.

About Life

See people when it comes to life a lot of us keep missing the point, like being grateful for what we have but still strive for what we want. We walk around with this attitude as if the world owes us something, but when it comes to volunteer or charity have you served or gave nothing. No matter how rich or healthy we can't survive in this world alone, though unfortunate things happen you will reap the benefits of what's sown. People often cry and ask why various tragedies has come their way, but there's a flicker of light in senseless acts which is a test of our faith. No one is exempt from hurt and pain but grief doesn't have to prevail, we're here for a purpose leaving a story to tell. Laughter, giving and patience is the spine to the essentials of living, while greed and bitterness deteriorates along with non-forgiving.

<u>Forgiveness</u>

It's the rebirth of the soul

Misinterpreted by pain's toll.

Seems impossible, remembering to forget

Internalized resentment leaves the skin thick.

But how will peace ever find its way

When bitterness eats the heart as it decays.

Conflicts at war of the heart and mind

Many restless nights you'll truly find.

Somehow you have to learn to let it go

Harboring it feeds the pain to grow.

It is the most crucial remedy in healing the heart

Though memories aren't erased Forgiveness is where it starts.

<u>Stones</u>

Judge me not as you cast the next stone

Shaking the heart assaulting loves' home.

Hear the whispering of rumors as gossip flies

Ignorance has blinded you from the beam in your eyes.

Selfish Love

Selfish Love look what you do to me

Reviving my heart to not set me free.

Just when I move on your hand I still hold

Inside I'm broke down again lost in the cold.

Your love went deep my all I surrender

Emotions up and down you're my contender.

If I ever catch you sleep to break out these chains

I'll never look back memories of pain.

Overdosed in misery your constant slave I was

Aware the dead can breath......Thanks to you Selfish Love!

How Do You Say You're Sorry?

How do you say you're sorry when you want this as just as much

Feeling the heart tremble at the thought of losing your touch?

How do you say you're sorry for letting fears get in the way

Not speaking and being stubborn, time wasted throughout the day?

How do you say you're sorry when your heart knows you're wrong

For going to bed with anger allowing the problem to prolong?

How do you say you're sorry when you've hurt the one you love

And you realize that you jeopardize what you both are made of?

As your friend and your mate I come with full regret

I don't want to lose your love and I cherish that we met!

<u>Passing Through</u>

If you seek to determine within the means of this earth

Your validity in identifying the extent of self-worth;

Then you repress to a minimum a great strength within

As deception surpasses this world pulls you in.

With each stride to survive in fulfilling your goal

The appearance may be elaborate as desolation eats the soul.

Don't allow riches and wealth to be gained in vain

We're Kings and Queens but know the name above all names.

Let no possessions to proudly define you,

This visit is brief....we are only Passing Through.

Why I Walk Alone

I enjoy company but choose to walk alone

My every move is judged as they throw words of stone.

I can't help but love them and from a distance I will

Alleviate bitterness Lord, I pray as I kneel.

Hearts so ungrateful and self-centered with no shame

An invite to a gathering but I regret that I came.

I long to be surrounded with laughter and good cheer

The plaque of gossip spreading, I cease to go near.

And the dark side of things is all they can see

But it corrupts the soul and it doesn't please me.

I'm grounded with serenity in the comfort of my home

Away from all the havoc….that's Why I Walk Alone.

Love Debts

When we met, we had nothing.....nothing but our hearts and with that to gain.....we were rich. All that others had to offer meant nothing.....for whatever was needed we found by ways of each other. With time baby..... we grew, and so did the world around us.....slowly allowing comfort to set in......so much comfort that the value of our love grew dim. How were we too blind to not see that we were losing love at the expense of comfort? What a great lost..... leaving hearts to pay the cost.

You're Gonna Wish

You're gonna wish one day you never left my side

That day you feel your heart has died

Yeah you're gonna wish that I were your bride.

All the times you spoke of love

And the future plans made for us.

Now I see the faceless dream

So real those lies seemed

I'm moving on to better things.

One day you're gonna wish

That you didn't miss so much my kiss

For all I gave I don't regret

But baby this ain't about that.

Look at this mess you've made

What we had again you'll crave.

While all the times you spoke of love

And future plans made for us

Now I see the faceless dreams

Oh so real those lies seemed got to move on to better things.

Countless times played with my mind

Took back my smile every time

Freedom has found me I'll be fine.

My love one day you'll truly miss

But for me no more of this

One day my love......You're Gonna Wish!

Silly Me

How silly to walk in another's path for them to lead the way,

For them it was successful but I was left astray.

Silly of me to think in our tender years that you'd stay true,

So blind, couldn't see it coming until my heart broke in two.

My silly thoughts once led me to think every day would be sunny,

But in life's journey of twist and turns at times nothing's funny.

Seek for yourself and don't believe everything one has to say,

Silly me placed all eggs in a basket and had nothing the next day.

They say to tell the truth, for it will surely set you free,

Now I realize the double standard in that…..No more Silly Me.

Familiar Stranger

In passing my eyes glanced though the face I hadn't really seen,

At that moment my soul awakened to this feasible reoccurring dream.

I questioned the introduction for your presence I perceive,

Who is this perfect stranger that is so familiar to me?

Through our conversation, getting more acquainted in hopes of curiosity to fade,

Long talks of past experiences, many hurts given and made.

So refreshed yet enlightened I felt more aware than before,

This awesome event that took place reevaluated me to the core.

So now when I look into the eyes the face is clear to see,

That familiar stranger I had partially known was that dark side of me.

In My Shoes

I'm not perfect, never said that I was

And whatever I do is just what I does.

Sometimes I'm impulsive, o.k. I'll admit,

But selfish and jealous that's not me one bit.

I'll give what I've got if that's what it takes,

And sometimes my giving is my mistakes.

You live and learn, hey that's just life,

Along with pleasure comes the pain and strife.

So when you speak on me, I have nothing to lose,

As I can recall you've never walked In My Shoes.

I Question Myself

I question myself as to why I'm still here, is it tenacity or loneliness I fear?

The more I give the more I lose you, this parachute of love is failing fate is overdue.

So no more watering weeds or beating a dead horse, what influence your love to reverse, I question the source.

All the while passion for you was in vain, in tears I questioned had you ever felt my pain?

Though all the signs were there I didn't care to look, denial flooded my mind and me for granted you took.

I question would I have changed a thing? To receive the love in exchange for hurt you bring.

I'll slowly move forward and come to terms with the past, unsure of love's commitment with another to last.

My soul's strength will mend this shattered heart you left, but invitation for love leaves me Questioning Myself.

Dear Karma

Dear Karma, I know this may come as a surprise

But indications of bias reflect in your eyes.

Is there a law in your nature I may have overlooked?

Either your ways are peculiar or you overbooked?

Because you always seem to be so preoccupied

I'm still waiting for my good deeds to be multiplied.

See I interpret your law as you reap what you sow

But it seems the bad out-weighs the good with your flow.

Could I be picking up the tab from generations before me?

Seems the harder I try the more odds are against me.

Deposits of kindness I've yet to seek in return

Only lessons of disappointments I've too often learned.

With all due respect Karma your game's a little twisted

By-passing everything but evil it's time you fess and fix it!

Karma's Come-Back

Hi this is Karma and I sense bitter in your tone

Placing the blame on me …..I won't condone.

My game's twisted? Oh no, it stays on point

You get what's put in so don't question me with your wants.

Life's another game and it may not seem fair

But don't hold me responsible for your despair.

So take heed in planting seeds and how they grow

I'm an equivalent response to your acts ….oh you didn't know?

The remnants of evil is always far more felt

These cards shuffled and cut are the ones you dealt.

To error is human, simply no disputing that fact

So don't sleep on my existence because Karma will Come-Back!

Runaway Heart

Rotating circles, in a maze

So confused in a daze, my runaway heart.....

Loves from afar, to protect its scar

Seek no more than what you are, my runaway heart.....

Fulfillment and desire tries to empower

But shadows of deception over showers my runaway heart.....

Gone to an undisclosed location

In preparation of a solo vacation, my runaway heart.....

Return date unknown, bad seeds had been sewn

When will you come home, my Runaway Heart?

HUMANITARIAN

I Wonder

Look Further

Cries

No Reason

Broken Silence

I'll Cry

Whispering Trees

What's Going On?

I Wonder

I wonder why joy comes with birth

Knowing the struggles of this earth.

Why isn't it a crime to throw food away?

When famish lives strong from day to day.

I wonder why we judge people that we don't know?

Has society somehow taught us so?

Why doesn't family matter anymore?

Could that be why children's values are poor?

And what's the harm of prayer in schools?

Fear of an antidote for the rising of fools?

I also wonder how we get peace from war?

Is it really worth all the killing for?

How can a parent abandon their own child?

So many lame excuses.....that's foul!

I look to Heaven when times get too rough

And can't help but wonder if he's had enough.

__Look Further__

Don't glimpse at my skin

But the heart within

And all that it offers

Ever if the tone is darker.

This silhouette you see

Isn't whom you've assumed it to be.

Tell Me:

Why do you seem to under-mind?

Perhaps intimidation haunts your mind?

Or does boldness of colors make you blind?

From the depths of my soul I've tried to understand

Why one perceives to be the greater man.

Such notions causes a heart to tremble in its chest

Because of beautiful tones great ones are laid to rest.

Cries

Neglect

A whimper, a moan, high pitched tones of a child abandoned left to fend on their own.

Wedding Day

Joyful tears emerged as the bride unveils, a bond is formed new chapters of their lives to tell.

Torture

Screams of agonizing pain sends chills through your vein, the heinous beating of open flesh so inhumane.

Newborn

Cries from a newborn oh so tender and warm, embraced with love as baby grow and form.

Misery

Cries in the dark of a silent broken heart, so stricken with grief feeling torn apart.

Every cry relays a message as to how it came about.......a reaction directly from the heart emotionally poured out!

No Reason

For no reason another life was taken

So abrupt did it have to end?

What fueled this act to commit such a sin?

The future for this person is now laid to rest

An opportunity stolen to expose their best.

Was it really that serious for murder to be committed?

All eyes on the killer, still No Reason why he did it.

Broken Silence

The burden, the scars…..You so well kept

The hidden face of abuse…..In the closet you wept.

A slave to pain…...And no hand to lend

For each day you died…..But you kept it in.

If silence could speak…..It would be the first to tell

How quick joy was forgotten…..For the embrace of Hell.

But there had to be an Angel…..Made especially for you

Breathing life into your soul…..Slowly bringing you through.

Everyday is recovery from the works of violence…..Gives more meaning to your life when there's Broken Silence.

I'll Cry

I cried when you were born, counting all fingers and toes

A true warrior, putting up a fight while trying to clean your nose.

Then time went by and before I knew it I was crying again

Oh yeah, it was your first day of school and you had made a friend.

The wonder years are gone and you're gaining control of your life

Concerned with anxiety, I pray to eliminate strife.

With dignity and honor you chose to protect our great home

And Lord knows I broke down when they said my baby was gone.

I keep memories of you with each day passing by

When my journey's over and we meet, my Angel, again I'll Cry!

*In memory of those who has passed

While serving our country. (USS Cole)

Whispering Trees

To: Elantra

As the roaring winds ceased and the whistling of air became calm

There stood vast multiple trees with branches posed like arms.

The Oak stood bold yet you could hear his plea for rain

Images of the dead slave's blood was left on its bark to stain.

Then the Pine tree's voice arose with a grisly story to tell

Many trees he exclaimed had witnessed this familiar act as well.

He wanted no part of the noose around the neck of the corpse that hung

The Pine felt so ashamed for being used for evil to be done.

Then you could hear the wrestling of leaves at the base of trees during silence

The Birch sighed, "When will they stop cutting us into burning crosses for violence?"

We were made for shade, paper and to furnish homes

Not to taunt and be used for bloodshed due to different skin tones."

"We help to provide a breeze and for animals to build a nest

If we could ever speak as a witness in court, I'm sure the verdict would rest."

The branch of the Maple fluttered as she came up with a wish for mankind

"Nature and Earth would be more at peace if all humans were born blind!"

What's Going On?

I'm here shaking in my bones because I'm sensing some trouble in our homes; and all I can do right now is sigh as I look to the Lord asking why? I hear of so pain and grief but see no signs of relief and why because there's a lot of Indians running loose with no chief.

What's Going On? ....Parents and Leaders this one's for you and I want you to take this personal because I do. Is the time taken to teach your child love, respect and discipline and when they come to you acting out are you really truly listening? Don't use money as an excuse to spend quality time, trips to the park, their school or library doesn't cost a dime.

Again I ask What's Going On? .....Now ask yourself is our house a healthy home? Why are our children in a rush to be grown?

Parents are you sure you're taking care of home? A clean place, paying bills and full course meals aren't the only things that keep a child emotionally fulfilled. Attention, love and patience a child needs from day to day, it's up to parents to fill this gap or our children will stray.

What's Going On? ....Leaders if your heart isn't in it for the cause then you don't need to be in it at all. Power and greed will only mislead causing our community to divide and fall. Our children flesh of our flesh and bone of our bone, let's get back to family structured homes and we will know What's Going On!

SPIRITUAL FAITH

I Wrote This

The Knock

So Help Me God

God's Love

The Storm

Keys of Redemption

In My Prayers

Seed of Faith

Lord, Forsake Us Not

Judgement Day

Truth

The Revelation

Clouds of Death

Ressurrected Me

Dip Me In the River

I Wrote This

To: My Fans

I wrote this from my tears which have fell a thousand times

From diverse emotions and a daily renewed mind.

I wrote this from abuse by others and myself

For healing from within as well as my health.

I wrote this as a gift I could find nothing greater

However, I do not write this without the hand of the Creator!

The Knock

Awaken by a knock as I rose out of bed

"Who is it?" I asked but no reply instead.

I headed back to my room irritated inside

Did I dream this or did someone knock and hide?

Giving it no more thought as many months went by

One night again came the knock so I took a deep sigh.

No one is at the door, is this a reoccurring dream?

I know I'm not hearing things it's too real it seems.

As I laid in silence with no intentions for sleep

Then arose in my heart a voice started to speak.

"It is I that knocked, for your prayers were in need,

How faithful is thy servant when you don't water your seed?"

"For there is work to be done and on many I will call

And those who don't answer will be the ones to fall!"

So Help Me God

Times are hard so help me God.

All this stress wearing on my flesh.

Focus my eyes upon you

As thicker clouds keep rolling through.

Please Lord grab my hand

Especially when I can't stand.

When my soul's screaming out

Rebuking all those lies of doubt.

Weeping endured many nights

Forsake me not, shine your light.

I'm losing strength, feeling weak

You're in need for shelter and sleep.

These times seem much too hard

I'm reaching for you, so help me God.

God's Love

The love that is bonded in me

Is greater than any man conceives.

Sometimes I'm even astounded

But I thank God that I found it.

It's a great treasure to own

Personally sent from Heaven's throne.

And I'll let it expand as it will

Spreading it to allow others to feel.....God's Love.

The Storm

I don't know what this world is coming to

Lost souls drifting by watching me, watching you.

Although I'm in this world I'm not of it

And sometimes I'm disgusted but still love it.

It's a constant struggle to not get entrapped

Makes me think sometimes I'm going to snap.

But I won't allow my mental to decline

Turning to my source for a sane mind.

As I methodically keep pressing through with it

Leave it in God's hand, he knows what to do with it.

<u>Keys Of Redemption</u>

Angels of darkness it's time you die

No more evil, deceit or tears to cry.

On to your wicked schemes and games

Rebuking by the power of Jesus' name

The fall of your kingdom brought down to shame.

By precious blood we so live

No more torture shall you give.

All is revealed the veil is uncovered

The Word is unleashed now your fire is smothered!

In My Prayers

As I went about the day a glimpse of you in my mind appeared

Then came a sense of urgency though the circumstances weren't clear.

I asked for the Angels to be brought forth for your shield and protection

That our Shepherd in troubled waters would lead your direction.

If dark shadows of loneliness come and you think he's forsaken you

David bears witness to God's Word in Psalm 22.

I pray you'll look to him in all things and clearly hear his voice.

And for abundant blessings to rain down and in the Lord we shall rejoice.

"Father, break any chains of bondage to affliction as serenity is restored

Replenish strength for this battle will perish and victory is ours says the Lord.....Amen."

<u>Seed Of Faith</u>

Lord, as I plant this seed of faith today

My hand I give as I follow your way.

This road is tough, seems no relief in sight

My faith knows our battles you'll fight.

When harm seems to have me all surrounded

I'll remember your promise to keep me grounded.

Though the pain at times is hard to bear

Lord touch my heart and I'll know you're there.

You're the greatest love we can't physically see

So I'll nourish this seed as it grows in me.

Lord, Forsake Us Not

I see the remnants of Satan's craft

Fear and hurt settling into wrath.

Though your love I cast not to the side

Seeking shelter as evil tries to hide.

Knowing mankind's destruction will only get worse

I painfully watch love ones leave in a hearse.

Now the structure of family is weak and thin

Grief fills my eyes and I'm weary within.

Sin spreading like wildfire out of control

Lost generations arise when parents don't fill their role.

Why blame the victims though the bite is vicious

When inside hurt explodes from the heart love misses.

"Lord, Forsake Us Not!"

Judgement Day

So you must like playing with fire

Wait until the return of the Messiah.

Echoes and screams of taunted souls

It's near see how this world's out of control?

They'll be nowhere to try and hide

You sleepwalkers better open your eyes.

For mercy will expire when the wrath gives way

Prepare your soul now for Judgement Day!

<u>Truth</u>

And I'm back....lips together please no debate

Spitting words in the airways to saturate

Your molecules, your cells

Yes, I'm here to water your wells.

I can't help but tell of his Glory

And the stories of those who rose before me.

So this is my Gift that I share with you

From Abba Father, the God-given Truth.

The Revelation

Let no man of this Earth be yet deceived, souls will vacate from its corpse no longer to be.

But before the trumpet is profoundly sound, death, mourning and pain will make its round.

Hungryfor knowledge and relief from the strain, cautious of the wisdom you seek it may be falsely gained.

Corruption has spilled upon the land into churches and homes, even nature's taking a stand against all the sin it's outgrown.

Dance not in hell's kitchen as the enemy draws near, be not afraid of satan but God's wrath you should fear.

The most greatest among us a Judas may reflect, seek God first and far-most and through his word he'll direct.

Plant deep the roots of the Spirit to dwell, embrace redemption through our Savior or your reward will be Hell….The Revelation!

Clouds Of Death

I feel the stings upon my flesh

By the rain from the clouds of death.

And though I may waver I shall not fall

My life is planned and it's his call.

Until my Divine destiny's fulfilled

A surrender to death is yet to yield.

Open death clouds as rain poured

By-passing fatalities was the work of the Lord.

You've watched over me Father as you did your Son

So I can proceed the work here to be done.

In tune with your Spirit as you guard every step

My life's umbrella from harmful clouds of death.

Resurrected Me

To: Taylin

Was cast so low, deep in a dark pit

Didn't know how I got there or back there how to get

Definitely didn't want to live like this.

The life I once knew faded away

Reluctant to face another strange day

So cold and rigid trying to find my way.

Felt like a complete waste

Of existence and energy, lost my pace

The loneliness and pain will it be erased?

What had I done......was a curse on my life?

And how did I become this monument of strife?

Lord, help me turn my wrongs into right.

So I turned a new page still lost in the struggle

Place my trust in him when encountered by trouble

For enduring he promised to give back double.

Ones that knew me aren't sure who I've become

Had a heart of stone and feelings were numb

But today I'm being that better someone.

Found life in the words of the Divine

Aware that my life alone isn't mine

Heavenly rays on me now shine.

Lord, I know it had to be you

Broke me in pieces to bring me through.

New life in my soul came from Thee

I'm in the land of the living the Resurrected Me!

<u>Dip Me In The River</u>

Dip me in the river that cleanses souls,

Yes the river yet to behold.

The distinct river that runs to and fro,

Cast into this wishing well what dreamers come to know.

Dip me the river in its gentle stretch-out hand,

As the waves glide hastily toward land.

Draw from the water life bestowed of the Giver

For blessed be thy name

As I'm dipped in The River.

The James River in N.N., VA

INSPIRATION

Do This

Yeah keep chasing your dreams though society wants you sleep

Hustling to survive barely surviving the hustle to make ends meet.

And to all my entrepreneurs……..talk is cheap, be doers.

With intentions to help out the next

Not in return for money or sex.

Send a prayer out when you're caught in the mix

And flip the down play to the upside and let's Do This.

Endurance

I seek endurance when the shadows of death is cast upon me

When my image is tainted by chants of mockery.

Endurance from temptation when trying to sustain

When the lost of love ones harbors pain.

Endurance when words that hurt suffocates my heart

And those silent cries that lingers alone in the dark.

Endurance to bare the eyes of evil that stare

And when I'm taken for granted yet continues to care.

Endurance to relentless stones thrown in my face

When my mind desperately seeks a resting place.

Endurance to forgive beyond unspeakable acts

When love replaces betrayal despite the fact.

Endurance when the bonds of love are somehow broken

Or deceptive rumors spread by crude words spoken.

When the voice of failure echoes and I lack assurance

Embed deep within me strength for Endurance.

<u>Claim It</u>

Yes

I manifest

To be bless

Nevertheless

Won't contest

To carry out destiny's quest

Aim high, never second best

For prosperity I confess

As seeds of faith and wisdom I digest!

<u>Solid Ground</u>

Look deep within to gain elevation, of your high expectations.

Don't let those to the left or the right succumb you the epitome of these industries.....

For your answers you won't find in the streets.

Be bold search your soul

Yet take heed to the good and evil that's around

Seek wisdom, serenity, and prosperity

So your foundation is Solid Ground.

<u>Dry Tears</u>

They have no clue what's going on inside

Playing the role concealing the hurt you hide.

A bright smile or maybe to them it seems

All the while you're wishing life were a dream.

A heart felt embrace and you thought you'd break

Really needing that hug but proceeded being fake.

"I'm doing fine." So convincing you say to your friends

A half laugh, the character you play to the end.

A true friend listens with their heart to hear

And says, "Let's heal the wounds behind those tears."

Entrepreneur

I'm an entrepreneur

An individual doer.

Where others see failure is where I strive

Taking a different approach in life to survive.

Sometimes looked upon as hopeless dreamers

But tenacity unfolds our visions as redeemers.

Rebirth of a Scorned Heart

I told myself I wouldn't cry, still the hurt I feel I can't deny.

I said I wouldn't bring it up again, the thought sticks in my head as it spins.

Forgiving isn't easy and forgetting is hard, reprogram my heart to create a new start.

I wish to be with you though blemishes get in the way, guide my path oh Lord through another hectic day.

Searching for serenity in things I can't change, and strength to love unconditionally with happiness to gain.

<u>In My Eyes</u>

In my eyes all colors will reflect

All walks of this economic intellect.

The youngest of years to the oldest

The fairness of skin to the boldest.

My nature connects with many souls

Any means to spread warmth when it's cold.

No I'll never walk in your shoes

Through ups and downs my love you'll never lose.

For in my eyes when I see you....I see me

That light shining in your heart is where I'll always be.

Remember Them Days

To: Mom

Remember….Plastic covered sofas, big afros, long fake fur coats, butterfly collars, Mom's home cooking while Pop's at work?

Recycled soda bottles, one line phones, no color T.V., brown paper bags, no ceiling fans or central A.C.

Remember….Jack rocks, double-dutch, train sets, hide 'n seek; corner store pickles, lemon heads, but no sweets before you eat?

Sponge rollers, gas stoves and sit down bath, every Sunday after church the family ate dinner, talk and laughed.

Remember….Teddy P, Al Green, the Delfonics, and high stacked shoes; record players, 8 tracks, juke joints singing to the Blues?

The Jefferson's, Sanford & Son, Good Times, and Soul Train, Dodge ball, Red light/ Green light as kids we'd play in the rain.

Remember…..Mom pierced our ears, straightening combs and home cooked meals; silk and polyester outfits riding on white-wall

wheels? "Respect your elders"…."Child, mind your manners"

Yes and no ma'am"….The biggest sleepovers ever because family's in from out-of-town.

The oldest child got more money while the youngest gets their way……and family always had each other's back….Ya'll Remember Them Days!

<u>Turning Point</u>

At which point do I turn and leave what we had behind

Aware of the wrongs we can't right, now running out of time.

If at one point I turn....I'd be a fool to stay

Love doesn't erase coldness you display.

Oh you say you still love me but can't go back in time

At that point I searched your heart and nothing was to find.

The depths of my heart's love for you is infinity

But there's a point in which I must turn to save my own identity.

I was weary and hurt when depression filled my joints

Then the epiphany of loving me first became my Turning Point.

<u>Ingredients of Love</u>

Something is brewing.......see I've been working on this dish, it doesn't require a recipe, a chef or list.

Step 1: Usually I'd preheat the oven, but in this case room temperature is fine.....today they'll be no interruptions as you and I spent Quality Time.

Step 2: I lick the bowl after mixing Trust and Honesty....They aid in nutrition and is healthy for you and me.

Step 3: Now don't forget to check on Intimacy, it has the tendency to come to a boil.....Then spread Respect all over and cover with foil.

Step 4: Let cool, then top with Communication, something we take advantage of.....It may not be obvious but those are the Ingredients of Love!

*If at first you don't succeed repeat steps 1-4.

INTIMATE MOMENTS

Before We Say Goodbye

I'll Be

Therapy

Never Knew

Take My Hand

Full Of You

Appeal

Bring Back the Love

My Chocolate Thunder

Sexual Emancipation

Gotta Make You Mines

Stay With Me

Love Again

Got This Feeling

Dream of Me

Never Intended

A Taste of My Soul

Before We Say Goodbye

This right here is a hard thing to do moving along can't believe we're through.

Sometime my mind wonders if it's a mistake whatever we kept doing this is our fate.

Thought we'd grow together in our days of old but the plot shifted as the story unfolds.

I dread the day seeing you with another .the death of a friendship and also a lover.

Hell yeah it hurts that we have to leave…but we haven't been happy, no indeed….bringing out the worst in you and me.

I'll take no more of your time wishing you the best remembering lessons learned from this beautiful mess.

As I turn to leave it's in my heart I cry…..I just had to let you know Before We Say Goodbye.

I'll Be

I'll be that lady you've wished all your life for

The missing one you'll seek no more.

I'll be that breeze that helps catch your breath

That nourishment best for your health.

I'll be that leg to support your stand

A faithful woman there for her man.

I'll be the finger to wipe away your tears

That gentle voice of reason, chasing away fears.

I'll be your helpmate and bring forth the word

I'll be your first lady, the second and third.

I'll support your movement keeping you on the rise

Whenever it is friction I'll compromise.

I'll be with you from beginning to the end

Always that great lover and forever your friend.

<u>Therapy</u>

I need a therapist.....physically

One who can work the anatomy?

Reaching muscle failure so passionately

While containing the fire burning in me

Until the work out is fully complete.

<u>Never Knew</u>

I thought you knew had figured it out

Just how I felt but no words came about.

Tried to get to your heart like you got in my head

Doing all the right things the wrong way instead.

You never knew just how I felt

Opening my heart each time love dealt.

Longed for your arms to hold but in your eyes I was so cold....because you never knew.

You thought I knewhad said it all

But I had no clueanother fall.

Couldn't see from hind sight when you flashed green lights

Signals mixed with fright so I bailed and took flight.

We never knew just how we felt

Chemistry so strong, things we can't help.

And we don't know what lies ahead

For Destiny is written and now it's being read....we Never Knew!

Take My Hand

Take my hand and never let go

And in your heart be still and know

What God has joined shall never part

It was done in Heaven and placed in our heart.

So take my hand and lead the way

Our eyes on God so our feet won't stray.

This love was built on solid rock

May Almighty eyes stay upon our flock.

<u>Full of You</u>

You stimulated my curiosity transpiring me to higher elevations

Your elements magnetize my essential being bringing forth sensations.

Never once you leave me longing for the enhance doses of your vibe

Yet within my appetite for you.....hunger still exist!

Now I'm taking a walk through the thoughts in my mind wondering what
is this?

Finding your perceptions overwhelming my thoughts seeping into the
depths of my dreams.

I walk to your pace....sing to your tune....Hell in every other conversation
I include you!

I know I'm not falling into this façade of being whipped....hold on yall I
know I need a sip!

In all aspects I find no fault in how I feel.....but only if this imagery
conception is real.

So do I soothe your soul.....take it to places it's never been before?

Do you ever question certain things you do? Or am I just Full of You?

<u>Appeal</u>

Trying to maintain composure as your presence draws close

Your persona capsizes my demeanor you're unlike most.

Though I'm very confident in this character I portray

The likeness of who you are eats through me right away.

Bring Back the Love

Bring back the love that we once had

The emotions shared that doesn't leave us sad.

Bring back the woman that you always dreamed of

Beautiful and honest, so full of love.

Bring to me that man, respectful and true

That man I met that I saw in you.

Together we stand facing our Father above

Asking in our hearts to Bring Back the Love.

<u>My Chocolate Thunder</u>

I'm in love with a man who says he loves me

When looking in his eyes a reflection I don't see.

I once captured his heart the way he has mine

But it seems to grow cold with the passing of time.

How can love so strong be built on quick sand

It was nothing I felt when I reached for his hand.

So now I'm stuck with this heart that knows only him

I'm in a pool of his love but I continue to swim.

I'm in love with a man and I can't help but wonder

If he's a chapter of my past or My Chocolate Thunder.

Sexual Emancipation

There's a long awaited anticipation stirring up inside, submerged with strong urges I seem to no longer hide. The virtuous thought of you caressing me sends sensual hot chills, my mind revolved in an illusional state uncanny to what's real. I'll sporadically spread poetry throughout your body with my tongue, as your flesh of fire passionately builds our bodies emerge as one.

In panting I sense yearning magnetically enticing my hunger, at the height of losing captivity for this bondage I can take no longer.

The gentle thrust of exertions transcends unspeakable stimulation, leaving my heart racing to the beat of Sexual Emancipation!

Gotta Make You Mines

It's been a while since I've felt this way,

Those sweet kisses and smiles just make my day.

Playing and laughing like kids do,

Love the mere fact of the beauty in you.

You know what to say and just how to say it,

If this were a game then forever let's play it.

Admiring you while you're sleep,

Your words of comfort stay with me.

I can't help the deep passion I feel,

Embracing this love as our heart heals.

Creating new melodies for us to sing,

In this circle of love joy will bring.

If you ever leave.... my sun won't shine,

What I'm trying to say is I Gotta Make You Mines.

<u>Stay With Me</u>

Sitting by the water thinking of what I should have said

Chest feeling heavy with things racing through my head.

Don't want to pay for letting you slip away

Swallowing my pride to ask for your return today.

Didn't take long to see the turn I made was wrong

Baby you and I are much too strong

Say you'll stay with me, this is how we belong.

Let's head to a place where we're not known

Feeling nothing but free so our love can roam.

I picture us lying in each other's arms

Rest assure my intentions has no harm.

It took my heart to write this song

Don't know why it took so long

Together is how we belong...

Say you'll Stay With Me.

<u>Love Again</u>

I lay awake in the wee hours thinking of you

Recapturing the events of things we used to do.

Vivid memories bring about a smile on my face

Though my heart know not love's place.

It's tricky with no one to guide or steer it

So the more I desire it the more I fear it.

During the rise and fall of me and you

I've also thought of loneliness too

Printed scars on my heart what else can I do?

I've given it my all hoping things would be right

Only to find I'm still alone at night.

Relinquishing the pain my heart's been through

Trying to believe in love like I once knew.

But this thing called love is a gamble to win

Bringing me to the thought.......if I'll Love Again?

Got This Feeling

It's been too many weeks and too many hours since I've seen your face or seen your smile, I want you to come on home.

I feel my soul burning with flames when I feel your touch or hear your name, when are you coming home?

I've been pacing the floor going from wall to wall checking my text and hoping you'd call, cause I've got this feeling.

I've got this feeling baby that I just can't seem to shake, how you love me when you do me that way....

I've got this feeling that I've been holding deep inside and I want to give it to youbecause you make me come alive.

I smell your scent when you're not around, I need your love I need it now.... please baby come on home.

My friends don't know what's wrong with me, got me so wrapped up in your ecstasy...I can't take this feeling.

I've been pacing the floor going from wall to wall, checking my text and hoping you'd call because of this feeling.

This feeling, it just won't leave my soul it's taking me hostage and it won't let me go.....Cause I've got this feeling baby that

I just can't seem to shake, how you love me when you do me that way.... and this feeling baby I've been holding deep inside and I've

Got to give it to you because you make me come alive.

Come on home come see about me....wanna hear your footsteps baby.... because I've got this feeling

Open the door wanna hear those keys....come on baby come rescue me.... because I've Got This Feeling.

Dream of Me

When you lay down

Dream of me

I want to be

All up in your sleep.

Let's dance to a new beat

Put love on play and hit repeat

Sounds good right there…..

You and me!

Never Intended

I never intended to love you, never intended to care

You walked into my life one day, and somehow you're still there.

Had no intentions for us, it was never in my hands

God planted something in me, seeing you more than just a man.

I never intended to know you or share with you my heart

Just when I think it's over we're right back at start.

So I ask God to show me the reason you came my way

He reminded me of a dream before we met that day.

I never intended to hurt you or bring confusion in your life

And I never intend to lose you......reveal if I'm his wife.

A Taste of My Soul

If I share with you my weakness…..Would you still acknowledge my strengths?

And in the areas I fall short…..Would you carry me that extra length?

If I share with you my spirit…..Could you reach within to see

The Creator that dwells within…..Is the greatest part of me?

And if I share with you my heart…..Would you protect it with all your might

Avoiding intentional hurt…..Regardless of how rough the flight?

If I share with you my life…..Would you leave the past behind

And look into the eyes of Heaven…..For true love to find?

If we share these valuable treasures…..Allowing love to have control

I would never cease to continue giving you….

A Taste of My Soul.

About the Author

Dionna Ophelia, a native of VA has written well over 100 poems to include literary art for cards, songs, occasions, and more. The astounding work composed of this up and coming Author brings such a diverse complexity of tasteful authentic poetic literature that advertently magnetizes. Gracing appearances at open-mic, class and family reunions, as well as other private and social events, Dionna Ophelia continues to enhance writings into other venues as she sets her pen in motion for more to come.

www.ingramcontent.com/pod-product-compliance
Lightning Source LLC
Chambersburg PA
CBHW020609300526
45785CB00021B/379